I0472570

Procrastination Ends Now:

12 Secrets to Boost your Productivity, Increase Motivation and Develop New Habits in 21 Days

Michael Zenstar

© Copyright 2015 by Michael Zenstar - All rights reserved.

This document is geared towards providing exact and reliable information in regards to the topic and issue covered. The publication is sold with the idea that the publisher is not required to render accounting, officially permitted, or otherwise, qualified services. If advice is necessary, legal or professional, a practiced individual in the profession should be ordered.

- From a Declaration of Principles which was accepted and approved equally by a Committee of the American Bar Association and a Committee of Publishers and Associations.

In no way is it legal to reproduce, duplicate, or transmit any part of this document in either electronic means or in printed format. Recording of this publication is strictly prohibited and any storage of this document is not allowed unless with written permission from the publisher. All rights reserved.

The information provided herein is stated to be truthful and consistent, in that any liability, in terms of inattention or otherwise, by any usage or abuse of any policies, processes, or directions contained within is the solitary and utter responsibility of the recipient reader. Under no circumstances will any legal responsibility or blame be held against the publisher for any reparation, damages, or monetary loss due to the information herein, either directly or indirectly.

Respective authors own all copyrights not held by the publisher.

The information herein is offered for informational purposes solely, and is universal as so. The presentation of the information is without contract or any type of guarantee assurance.

The trademarks that are used are without any consent, and the publication of the trademark is without permission or backing by the trademark owner. All trademarks and brands within this book are for clarifying purposes only and are the owned by the owners themselves, not affiliated with this document.

Cover image provided by: (Provide image origin if needed)

Table of Contents

Introduction

If you have found yourself postponing important tasks over and over again, you are procrastinating. However, you are not alone. Most people procrastinate to some degree, but some of them are so chronically impacted by procrastination that it prevents them from exploiting their potential, and it has become a major obstacle in their careers.

Note that chronic procrastinators usually hold misconceptions regarding the reasons they procrastinate. You can ascertain this argument if you procrastinate because one reason you keep on postponing a task is that you want to do it perfectly. Holding onto this belief will not get things done.

Therefore, you need to understand that procrastination isn't linked to perfectionism, but rather to impulsiveness, which is the tendency to act on urges, as ascertained by Piers Steel, a professor of organizational behavior at the University of Calgary.

Some people perceive anxiety as the primary cause of delay in getting things started while others claim that they leave tasks to the last minute because they work better under stress. Whichever the reason you procrastinate, you need to know that consequences of chronic procrastination can be detrimental: loss of jobs, marriage break ups, feeling like an impostor, and more.

But how do you stop procrastinating? Do you just wake up one morning, think of yourself as an active, can-do person who can seize opportunities and solve problems? Well, let's admit the fact that everyone procrastinates: we all put off tasks.

However, according to research done by Joseph Ferrari, Ph.D., a psychology professor and Vincent DePaul Distinguished Professor at DePaul University in Chicago, 20% men and women are extreme procrastinators. They delay at work, in relationships, at home, and school. In fact, they have made it a way of life, and I will not be wrong if I call them 'waiters.'

Dealing with procrastination isn't an easy task, but this book will make it easier for you. But before we start displacing the procrastination in you with productivity, let's picture this; let's ensure that the obese people stop overeating, depressed individuals avoid apathy, and tell the beached whales that they are supposed to remain in the ocean.

Please note that "avoid procrastination" is an ideal advice for fake procrastinators – like someone saying, "I go on Twitter a few times each day – I'm such a procrastinator!" these people will shamelessly tell a chronic procrastinator, "just stop procrastinating and you will be all right."

One fact that neither fake procrastinators nor the dictionary comprehends is that for a chronic procrastinator, postponing tasks is not optional. It is a behavior that appears to be encrypted in them, and unless they find a way of decrypting it, they can't stop procrastinating. This book is a perfect tool to help the chronic procrastinators to boost their productivity and increase motivation in 21 days.

Let's get started.

Chapter 1

Understanding Procrastination

The dictionary explanation of the verb procrastinate is "to defer, put off, postpone, or prolong." The word originates from joining two Latin words: 'pro' which means 'forward' and 'crastinus' meaning 'belonging to tomorrow.' In simple terms, procrastination implies 'I will do it later.'

It is important to understand that procrastination is like a dandelion plant. You can try to uproot it and think that you eliminated it, only to realize that its roots are deep, and it just grows back. For some individuals, procrastination is like a flower that can be removed easily. To others, it is like dandelion whose roots are tangled and go deep into the ground. Note that these roots develop simultaneously, interweave, and shape each other as they grow. Therefore, we will discuss each root independently.

The emotional roots of procrastination involve fears, memories, hopes, doubts, dreams, inner feelings and pressures. However, you may not understand that these aspects have made you a procrastinator because you use procrastination to avoid uncomfortable emotions.

Underneath such delay and disorganization, you will be afraid that you are unacceptable in some way. Note that as painful as it is to judge yourself for procrastinating; self-criticism can be tolerated easily as compared to the feeling of vulnerability that is associated with trying so hard then land in the territory of fears. This is an uncomfortable territory but if you start evading your emotions, emotional imbalance sets in and you start looking for a way in a field of buried emotional land mines, afraid of stumbling into the next explosion.

To uproot this cause of procrastination, you need to understand your fears. Could it be fear of failure, fear of being controlled, fear of success or fear of intimacy? Sometimes it could be fear of separation in relationships. If only you can understand what you feel and how you feel it, you can become more confident and at ease with yourself. With that, you can be sure to start your tasks without procrastinating.

The second root of procrastination is one's complicated relationship to time. A procrastinator has a 'wishful thinking' approach to time. He perceives time as an opponent to outwit, outlive, or outmaneuver. If this is the way you perceive time, you are fuelling more procrastination.

Note that the moment your 'subjective time' conflicts the 'clock time,' it becomes difficult for you to work steadily toward an objective, anticipate deadlines, or estimate how much time you need to complete a given task. Also, your conflicting sense of time can create problems in your relationships with other individuals whose subjective time is aligned with the clock time. You might be tempted to procrastinate more if you are conflicting with others about time.

The biological root of procrastination is the third in our discussion and includes your brain, body, and genetic inheritance. I know you think this is weird, but you should understand that your body, brain, and genetic inheritance have a hand in your procrastination tendencies.

Neuroscience field has made some exciting discoveries that can help you to comprehend procrastination better. Timothy A. Pychyl, Ph.D., a professor of psychology at Carleton University and the author of The Procrastinator's Digest: A Concise Guide to Solving the Procrastination Puzzle, explains that the way we think can cause procrastination.

Pychyl explains that the limbic system, the most dominant portion of the human brain, is automatic. It tells you to pull your leg away from flames and also to ignore or flee unpleasant tasks. In simple words, limbic system directs you to opt for the 'immediate mood repair.'

According to Pychyl, the prefrontal cortex is a weak part of the human brain, but it plays a very crucial role – enables you to integrate information and decision making. It is the brain section that distinguishes humans from other animals that are controlled by a stimulus. However, the prefrontal cortex is not automatic, and you must kick it into gear to get things done. The moment you are less engaged in a task your limbic system is likely to take over and lead you to what 'feels good as at that time' – you procrastinate!

Therefore, if you have to end procrastination, collecting information about it without any other action will not help. You have to outsmart this habit of perpetually postponing stuff: trick yourself into productivity.

The interpersonal roots of procrastination touch on your social relationships, family history, and more. Sometimes, your past family dynamics may continue into the present day and could be playing a role in perpetuating procrastination that no longer serves you. Also, cultural and social concerns can contribute to your tendency to procrastinate and therefore, it is crucial to comprehend the influence of these factors on your relationship with others.

For you to succeed in ending procrastination in 21 days, I encourage you to understand the biological, social, and emotional roots of procrastination without blaming or criticizing yourself.

The Cycle of Procrastination

I was once a victim of chronic procrastination, and as I was recovering, I realized that this habit of postponing tasks has a life of its own. I can compare the experience of procrastination to living on an emotional roller coaster. Procrastinators' moods will heighten and fall as they attempt to make progress, yet they slow down naturally. When they start a project and work towards its completion, procrastinators tend to undergo a sequence of feelings, behaviors, and thoughts. We can call this sequence the 'cycle of procrastination.'

Each procrastinator may have a unique cycle which can be drawn within a period of weeks, months or even years. Sometimes, the cycle can manifest so rapidly that you move from the beginning to end within a few hours.

1. I will start my project early this time

At the start, you are usually very hopeful. As you begin a project, there exists a possibility that you will get things done in a systematic way. Though you feel unable to start straight away, you keep on hoping that you will start the project spontaneously. It is after realizing that time has elapsed that you discover you are not different, and your hope changes to apprehension.

2. I have to start soon

The time to start your project early is gone, and the illusion of doing your work systematically is fading. At this time, your anxiety takes over and the pressure to start your project intensifies. Since your hope of spontaneous start is gone, you now start feeling it's like you are being pushed by uncontrollable force to do something about the project. "But the deadline is not in sight." You say. "So, I still have hope and time, and I can get things done."

3. what if I don't start?

As time elapses, you haven't started your project, and you are no longer concerned about ideal beginning or even the force pushing you to start. The optimism in you is being replaced by foreboding.

You become entangled in the thoughts that you will never start your project, and you start visualizing how horrible the consequences are. At this point, you will feel paralyzed, helpless, and hopeless. Self-blame fills your mind, and you start condemning yourself while hoping no one finds outs that you haven't started the project.

4. Something is wrong with me

Now you are desperate. The good thoughts of beginning the work early failed. Guilt, shame, and self-blame didn't make you start on the project either. Now, the heightened worry to get the work completed is replaced with a more frightening fear: something is wrong with me!

This is the time you will feel that you lack the fundamental aspect of human life that everyone has – courage, luck, self-discipline, or brains.

5. the last choice: to do or not to do

This is the final decision a procrastinator has to make regarding the work at hand. You can either carry on to the bitter end or abandon the capsizing ship.

Some procrastinators will say "I can't stand this! And why to bother?" when you start reasoning in these lines, just be sure that you are not going start the project. After all, it is too late for you start. "I will start early next time," you whisper to yourself – a chronic procrastinator.

Not all procrastinators give up on their projects. Sometimes you may feel that you can't wait any longer and jumpstart your project. The consequences of giving up the project could ruin your life, and such thoughts can get you started on your project. Whichever the reason that forces you to start your work, you are still a procrastinator and you need to end this habit of putting off tasks over and over again!

The procrastinator's code

Every project I undertake should run smoothly and effortlessly.

I must do everything perfectly

It's safer to do nothing than to attempt and fail

If can't do something right, it's not worth trying

I should avoid being challenged

If I succeed, someone may get hurt

If I do well this time, I will always succeed

Following one's instructions means that I'm giving in, and I am not in control

There must be a right answer, and I will wait until I get it.

Does this sound familiar to you? These are assumptions that pave a way for procrastination. For example, if you think that you should do everything perfectly, then it's safer to procrastinate than attempting and risk failure. In the worst case, if you think your success is going to hurt other people, then, procrastination is the solution.

My friend, if you are still making the above assumptions, don't stop reading this book because all these assumptions are going to be replaced by productivity goals within the first 21 days.

So far, you have understood what procrastination is, what causes it, and how it manifests. Do you think the advice 'stop procrastinating' can end this weird habit of postponing tasks including cleaning your bedroom? You need a well-calculated approach to end procrastination and replace it with productivity. Check the next chapter for 12 secrets to boost your productivity, increase motivation and develop new habits in 21 Days.

Chapter 2

Enthusiasm: Your Ultimate Weapon in the war against Procrastination

We are done talking. It is time to stop this weird behavior of fiddling with miscellaneous things checking the latest posts on social media, watching videos, and loitering aimlessly when you have looming deadline. You have to stop squandering your free time and postponing important tasks till it's too late.

Enthusiasm is what makes the difference between achieving your goals and giving up before you start. Thomas Edison once said, "if the only thing we leave our children is the quality of enthusiasm, we would have offered them an estate whose value cannot be calculated."

When his research laboratory burned he was 67 years and as the fire cleared his popular 'inventory factory,' Edson told his children to go and get their mother because she will never set her eyes on a bigger fire than that. He was aware that enthusiasm is the perfect antidote for tragedy and the most powerful weapon to fight procrastination.

Note that the level of enthusiasm has nothing to do with your feelings; your feelings wake up on different sides of the bed each day. Therefore, to take control of your life, you must choose how you feel and not grant your feelings permission to control you.

We should not forget that discouragements, negative mindset, failure or overwhelming work can kill enthusiasm. Therefore, if you want to maintain your enthusiasm at a higher level and leave no room for procrastination, do the following.

• Stay away from people with a negative mindset. The people you associate with tend to influence your perceptions regarding various issues. Attitudes are contagious, and you keep close to people with negative mindsets, you will never stop procrastinating.

Instead, you will be exploring the mantle of procrastination. If you associate with positive thinkers, you will also become a positive thinker, confident, and develop enthusiasm.

• Schedule difficult tasks for the time of the day or week when your energy levels are high. This will ensure that the most important and difficult tasks are done perfectly and at the right time. You can focus on the less strenuous tasks after tackling the most strenuous and important ones.

• Tackle a task that has been a thorn in your side. When you start getting this done, your enthusiasm increases. Note that inactivity is a primary cause of depression and anxiety and this can make you not to work.

• Whenever you breeze through a project with particular competence and ease, analyze the factors that might have contributed to your productivity. Observe yourself each day for 21 days and you will develop a certain pattern. Use this pattern to schedule your tasks accordingly and you will be surprised how productive you will become.

Keep in mind that enthusiasm is a choice and is not a genetic inheritance. Mark Twain once pointed out that do something each day that you don't want to do. He perceived this is like the golden rule of acquiring the habit of doing your duty without pain. No one will ever make this choice for you.

Chapter 3

Conquer fear to end procrastination and stress

You cannot deny the fact that you have been postponing the tasks that you are afraid of. Well, everyone experiences fear at some point in their lives. However, if you evade situations and events that terrify you yet they are part of your responsibility, then, your fears have grown out of proportion, and you are procrastinating!

Note that there is a perfect way of overcoming fear especially in your line of duty: you must do what you fear. Attempting what you fear boosts your confidence, triggers enthusiasm, and productivity starts replacing procrastination.

For example, if you are afraid of preparing the cash flow statement for your company yet you are the accountant, grab the task, arm yourself with the necessary tools and DO IT! Whether you make mistakes all do it correctly, at the end of the day you will have to present a concrete cash flow statement. Soon, you will be laughing at fears that prevented you from becoming what you wanted to become.

Do you know that procrastination could be one of the key causes your stress? Throughout the history, great thinkers have indicated a relationship between the failure to act and the increasing levels of anxiety. For example, William James, an American Philosopher once said, "nothing is as fatiguing as the eternal hanging of incomplete task." Therefore, the more you postpone your tasks, the heavier you anxiety becomes. It will continue to become heavier till you complete the hanging task.

Establish objectives, prioritize them and measure your progress to overcome procrastination. You can consider breaking your goals into small milestones and achieve each at a time. This will boost your confidence and develop curiosity and the desire to achieve more.

To track your progress, ask your colleagues and friends for feedback. Reward yourself whenever you achieve a set goal, and if you fail, analyze the possible causes of failure and ask for guidance from your colleagues, mentors, or superiors. Then, try again while avoiding the pitfalls. With that, you will overcome the fear of accomplishing your responsibilities.

It is crucial to be honest with yourself when estimating how long it will take to do something you dislike or afraid of. If you run a grocery shop, I don't expect you to take a whole week to clean it once. Or if you are a PHP programmer, you can't allocate 12 months to coding software just because you are afraid of making mistakes. Therefore, allocate enough time to get the task done effectively.

Chapter 4

Planning will help you to Conquer Procrastination

Benjamin Franklin, a man who knew how to conquer procrastination once, said that "By failing to plan, you are preparing to fail." But how can I plan my work? A good question but I will ask you another heavy one; how will you know if you are achieving your goals if you don't plan?

Regardless the size of the project, a work plan is very important. Write down all the tasks that you have been putting off at your workplace. Not just the huge projects but the small ones as well. Also, make another list of the tasks you have been postponing at home. If you can't remember the small projects you have been putting off at home, just walk around in your home, and you will note the small projects you have been talking about but never began them.

Also, write another list of the things you have neglected in your personal relationships. This could include phone calls, family trips, vacations, visits and more. Lastly, write a list of the things that you have been putting off for yourself – an exercise program you should start, a class you need to attend, or a bad habit you want to end.

While writing these lists, don't worry about what to prioritize and what should take the backseat. Just list everything that comes to your mind. The main aim here is to capture all the tasks you have been putting off, and you will be surprised how one idea is likely to trigger the next. This will help you to recognize procrastination as a problem. Most procrastinators go to ridiculous depths to explain their habits of not acting. However, if you want to overcome this weird behavior, you have to accept procrastination as a problem.

After listing all the tasks, you have been postponing, ask yourself, "how much time do I waste in a day?" keep a record of how you spend your time. Also, check the plan you usually make to ensure that your deadlines are met: is it realistic? Are the goals achievable? Sometimes we tend to set unrealistic goals, and if we include such objectives in our daily work plans, we feel overwhelmed, motivation disappears, and procrastination could become an easy choice.

Before planning for each task, find out if the work needs to be done. Sometimes, you waste a lot of time on tasks that don't contribute to the success of your projects. Note that various tasks can be postponed justifiably. For example, visiting a friend and completing a client's project that is due in three days, what should be a priority?

Now that you what you have been postponing, how much time you waste in a day, and what should be a priority, you can schedule each task efficiently. Utilize planning tools such as to-do list to set small daily or weekly milestones and ensure that you complete each successfully.

Note that failing to act is what breeds doubt, doubt gnaws at your self-confidence, and your low self-confidence increases your indecisiveness. This leads to paralysis, and the vicious circle of inactivity continues. However, accepting procrastination as a problem, get to know what you have been postponing, and focusing how and when it can be done will trigger a series of actions. Most successful people know this secret: if you fail to plan, you are planning to fail!

Chapter 5

Overcome Procrastination: Accept Responsibility

You procrastinate because you delude yourself. Whenever you procrastinate, you deny reality and refuse to accept the responsibility for your life. If you want to end procrastination, you have to stop playing games with yourself and accept the fact that you are responsible for what you make of your life. Though this may be more honest than most people are capable of, but there is no other option to live a richer life.

We are responsible for all our actions, behavior, and thoughts whether deliberate or unintentional. Note that no one who can claim that he never makes a mistake, however, when a responsible person makes a mistake, he takes the responsibility and make it right.

"But how do I become a responsible person?" you ask. These tips will help you.

• Be accountable. If your coworker is unbearable, children feisty, or partner unreasonable, you are responsible for how you respond. Do you postpone tasks because your colleague is intolerable? Your behavior is under your control.

• Stop blaming you already know what needs to be done. It's one you stop pointing a finger at yourself you realize that you can control what you do. Just because a colleague is acting a fool, you don't have to be one to yourself.

• Acknowledge what a happened. Sometimes we make mistakes, but it's not good to cover them by making up silly excuses. You forgot to call your sponsor and instead of explaining how busy you were, find out how you can correct the mistake.

Accepting responsibility will enable you to make better decisions, keep small problems from becoming bigger ones, learn from your past mistakes, and strengthen your relationship. Also, acting responsibly will make you more productive and end procrastination.

Chapter 6

Motivate yourself to overcome procrastination

Marking a task in your to-do list 'done' brings with it a sense of freedom. To a procrastinator, it is a battle conquered - that work which was started but has taken longer than it should have. It may be minor, but crossing it as 'completed' is one of the most liberating feelings you can experience.

Jack Canfield in his book titled, "The Success Principles", suggests that the faster you move through the incompletes, the more attention units will be availed to the things that will bring significant changes in your life. Note that nothing beats the feeling that comes with shortening your to-do list. You will feel recharged. Here is how to get those stalled projects on course again and stay motivated.

• Eyes on the crown

Think about the results of the accomplished task. Once the project is completed, what are the gains? It helps to focus on the expected rewards after the job is done. The motivation pumps in more energy that will help you press on.

Even if the completion of the job or task reward is just that, completion, the feeling of freedom experienced when the task is done brings tranquility. More energy is then released to tackle new projects hence growth.

• Count the losses in shelving the task

How much do you stand to lose as long as the task is still on hold? Counting the losses will help you face the consequences and make you spring to action. The loss might be financial, emotional or social. Any loss is detrimental and scares anyone.

A trip down memory lane would also help. Assess the effects of something that was left unfinished in the past and with an honest mind evaluate the damage. Such acts affect other people in your circle as well.

- Take charge of yourself

Call yourself to a meeting and lay down some rules. Pay attention to the task at hand and ensure that you complete or are dedicated to complete it. Imagine yourself as tied to your desk or any other place that the task is to be done and you will become free as soon as you finish the task.

However, this calls for inner strength, focus, and self-discipline. Dealing with yourself ruthlessly will help you.

- Throw in something exciting

The brain can shut down at the thought of a boring task. To trigger the brain to excitement, try and engage in something you love while doing the project. This can be listening to your favorite artist or song, drinking your preferred drink or eating the meal you love. A place you love to visit can also do the trick.

- Identify the barriers

It is crucial to know what is stopping you from carrying out what is expected. There are different things, but these are the main ones; Ignorance on how to tackle it; overwhelmed or lack of clarity.

This is how you tackle the above:

Ignorance: Ask for help on how to execute the task

Overwhelmed: start with the small tasks

Lack of Clarity: start with what you easily understand

- Start

Do not wait to be ready as it may never happen. Once you set off the rest of the journey seems doable. You will never know how far you can go until you take the first step.

Chapter 7

Overcoming Procrastination: Block out distractions

Have you ever realized that willpower is among the limited resources that can be depleted just like any other form of energy? Just the way a morning jog can tire you for an evening jog, if you spend more energy while resisting temptation, you will have less energy to resist temptations later on.

Sometimes it is hard to focus on the work at hand especially if it's something that you don't want to do. Does this sound familiar? The situation can become worse such that even a quick distraction can derail your productivity. With that, you can find yourself postponing tasks and courageously say, "I will start this project tomorrow."

Blocking distractions can minimize procrastination and eventually end it. Therefore, if only you can avoid distractions, it could be a big step towards replacing procrastination habits with productivity mindset. Here are some of the tips to block distractions.

Hide or block distracting apps and websites

Parental controls are not just for the naughty kids – they are also handy for the distracted adults. If you are handling a project and at the same time receiving notifications from Facebook, Twitter, and other social networks, you need parental controls. These notifications will distract you, and you won't concentrate as expected.

Therefore, it is important to find a way of putting off such distraction. Consider removing the bookmark from your browser or uninstalling the app from your phone. Also, you can have a separate browser for work and another for social networks. For more drastic measures of blocking sites, use browser extensions such as LeachBox for Firefox and StayFocused for Chrome to block websites that distract you.

Keep distracting colleagues at bay

If you have ever worked in an open-layout office, you already know the right meaning of 'distractive co-workers.' Often, you have to deal with a chatty colleague, co-workers hooting questions that can wait, and other distracting issues.

A nice pair of headphone can go a long way in saying, "I'm busy now." If this does not help, don't hesitate in telling your co-workers that you are working on something that requires much attention. Also, consider giving them something to keep them busy as a way of blocking distractions.

Train your brain to focus

No matter how much you block distractions using headphones or telling your co-workers to keep off your office for some time, your brain can be the worst enemy. If it keeps on jumping from thought to thought when you have work to do, you need to control it. Otherwise, you will find yourself putting off tasks over and over again.

Chapter 8

Set Major Goals and Mini Steps

You cannot wake up, pack a bag and set off to an unknown destination. It does not happen. But sadly, this happens a lot in life. A lot of people sail through life with no particular direction. To them, goals are just where you wish to be.

Successful people in whichever area are known to set goals. Sometimes, goals can be wishes without having plans on how to reach the destiny, which is your goal. Such objectives can never be achieved. It is worth noting that to get to the peak of a mountain can be a lifetime highlight and one's dream, but the small calculated and tactful steps up are what make it possible.

The magnitude of the goal or dream can intimidate you and make you have another excuse to put the dream on hold. However, breaking it down to small, sensible phases make even the wildest dreams approachable and you will not feel any difficulty while conquering the small milestones.

This is so encouraging especially to someone who has procrastination tendencies. The small wins help rejuvenate you for the journey. As a human being, one achievement propels you to the next task as positive results are motivating on their own. Before you know it, you will have conquered major milestones and closing into your dream.

Setting goals and the mini steps also help distribute resources evenly. Planning here plays a major role. Time is distributed evenly, and cases of burn out can be avoided. For example, an individual would dedicate 2 hours every day to work out in a gym. The goal would be to achieve a certain size or lose a specific number of calories. The body is therefore not subjected to inconsistent hours of work out each day. Time is also distributed evenly without compromising on other things.

Progress is crucial in life. With small steps taken consistently, the people you interact with will notice the changes. Just the fact that someone noticed you have killed some inches on the waist one month into training is encouraging enough to keep you going. The temptation to procrastinate will be stifled as one feels the audience growing. No one wants to throw in the towel in public. Not when the results are positive.

Small steps help us grow in resilience and discipline. A total 180-degree change can be a tall order. Someone struggling with waking up 2 hours earlier may forever struggle to achieve that. Deciding to throw the blanket away when the alarm goes off may happen the first three days then the old slips in and conquers again on the fourth day. How about setting the alarm 20 minutes earlier for a week, then adding 20 more minutes for the next week until we get to our 2 hours goal?

Expecting that sudden overhaul may make procrastinating appealing again. Small steps, however, will inculcate discipline, creating resilience as well. This will also make the changes more stable as one progresses slowly but steadily.

Setting major goals and breaking them into shorter plans makes it more achievable and exciting. It appeals even to a procrastinator since the small tasks are more captivating.

Chapter 9

Pre-commit to overcome procrastination

When dealing with procrastination, pre-commit is one of the best approaches. Pre-committing serves as a debt of service, and debt has to be paid.

A common occurrence; the night before the exams you hear of students who can suddenly push themselves to trans- night and managed to memorize all the formulas and notes in a night. It comes through as a major achievement then.

Cramming is necessitated by the need to have crucial tasks that had been on hold for a long time done as there is no other option. Forget the sigh of relief when the crash approach action worked, quality is compromised in such an approach. The wise students would start there preparation for the exams early.

Still using the exams scenario as a case study, all through the studying, exams are inevitable. A student would, therefore, help themselves by laying down some sensible goals to help achieve the desired grades. This applies to other projects in life as well.

Thanks to technology and creativity, there is now an app known as StickK that can help anyone struggling with procrastination using a pre-commit approach. With this app, you set a goal after paying some money that will be held by the application, and you set a deadline by which you are to submit the project you are committing to.

If the task is not submitted by the set deadline, then the money is forwarded to a charity or a course that you hate. This acts as a motivation to make you work on the assignment as you stand to lose your hard earned cash to something you hate! An interesting approach, isn't it? You can also choose to have the cash passed on to something or an organization you would love to support.

The wake-up call here is the cost of procrastination – loss money. It may happen for the first time, but you cannot afford to keep on contributing money to a charity organization, due to jobs you should have done.

The other approach is a tested one that has proved true; the power of written words. Research proves that the people, students in this case, who write down the place and how they will complete a project were likely to do it.

It helps to write down how and the time frame for every project. The fact that you wrote it would haunt you any time you come across or think of it. Pre-committing through writing ignites a fire within, helps one focus and stands as a constant reminder.

Have an accountability person. It can be a spouse, friend, teacher or just anyone. Sharing your plans with someone is another great pre-committal step that makes us spring to action. The fact that there is some expectation from someone else other than you will help to set you rolling.

Human beings have the natural urge to protect their image. When you open up to someone else, you will want to live up to their expectation, which is to complete the task when you need to.

You can also decide to pre-commit by sending a notification to the relevant party when to expect the task. For example, sending a text to a client stating when they will get there order is a pre-commitment that will force you to work hard to do just that. Deliver on the promised time.

Chapter 10

Understand the 4 pillars of procrastination

We all know that procrastination can be a huge setback. It is a vice that even the victim would wish to get rid of. People who are mot struggling with the habit may be quick to brush off procrastination as an excuse. It is not. Studies have revealed that there are pillars of procrastination and identifying the various pillars would help you know how to conquer this habit. Let us face it; no one wants to shelve important things to a later date and rush through the task amidst deadline pressures.

1.   Low task value. We all love generous rewards and the value of the completed task most of the times, is the driving force. It is the motivation behind the urge to finish and get 'paid'. When the reward is nothing to write home about, the task becomes an energy sucker. All is not lost, though, you can decide to add some thrill to doing the task. If tasked with a boring article, sipping your favorite drink as you go about it can help balance the feeling.

It may also help to do the assignment in your preferred place if the nature of the work allows. This will contribute to exciting some part of you and pump some excitement into accomplishing the task.

2.   Nature of the person. It is proven that some people are unfortunately born procrastinators. They are just more likely to procrastinate since it is in them. Such people also seem to be easily distracted and hardly focus on the right things.

All is not lost, though. If you fall under this group of people, then all you need to do is take charge of the working environment. Ensure that where you set yourself to work has no or minimal chances of distractions.

Like for example, if pop-ups from the internet would easily lead you to click the cursor and peep what is happening on the social media page, get an app like StayFocusd. An application that blocks those tempting messages will be a worthy investment for you. In short, intentionally work to create an environment that will not encourage you to slip easily into procrastination.

3.   Be expectant. With high expectation, you are bound to stay focused and push yourself a little harder. The experience can, however, dampen the excitement of accomplishing the task, especially if not much came from the previous successful completion.

It is crucial to entertain positive thoughts of the assignment at hand and just get started. Sometimes the fear of starting keeps us from doing anything.

4.   Goal failure. Any task can be daunting with the fear of failure haunting you. Shedding off the fear of failure is vital as many people never get started imagining the result is nothing to be excited about. Why would you even start if you are sure you it is a futile attempt anyway? For many people with the habit of procrastinating, fear is a major setback.

Short term goals with unreal deadlines may help dilute this fear in a big way. The small progressive steps are a real catalyst to success.

Chapter 11

Practical Fantasies and Dream Big

Fantasies are normal in moderation. It is okay to step out of the world, into a new one that is perfect and experience how the ideal life should be. Who would not want that?

The flip side of extreme fantasizing however is, it can stifle achievable dreams. That perfect picture in your mind may overwhelm you into shelving the entire project for the fear of falling short of achieving what you have in mind.

Fantasies tend to focus on the wishful result and ignore the path that leads to the perfect place imagined.

According to research, the people who spent most of their time dreaming end up doing very little to get there and are poor performers when it comes to the actual execution. They seem to be comfortable holding onto the imaginations. It soothes or massages your persona and holds you back from forging on to the implementation bit.

This may be confusing as we are always encouraged to dream. Dreams motivate and propel us to the right direction – the essential part everyone should include in working towards the dream part in the fantasy.

For example, if one is dreaming or fantasizing about visiting a certain holiday spot, it is okay and advisable to think about what steps can lead to the realization of the dream. This is a healthy way of dreaming, and it has proven to show positive results.

The importance of visualization prior has been cited as:

Visualizing the process helps in planning. The visual picture helps draw a map in the mind on how to reach the desired results. It, therefore, helps to avoid unnecessary trial and errors that may easily encourage procrastination.

Planning also helps dispel the impossibility of a task and reduce it to 'chewable' pieces. When a plan is in place, resources are well utilized as they are pumped into the very deserving undertakings.

With planning, one can be assured of expedited journey to reach the goals by minimizing on the procrastination stop-overs.

Anxiety is greatly reduced with visualization. As human beings, when we walk the path again and again in our minds, our confidence is boosted and anxiety levels minimized. Imagine having to perform a piece or present a project in front of masses in the near future. Many people find themselves visualizing and acting the scene alone but imagining the audience is watching.

After some practice sessions with the imaginary audience, it becomes less terrifying. The anxiety will most likely not disappear because of this, but will be manageable to the majority.

Fantasy helps to keep dreams alive and hopeful. It gives the heart some warmth to know that there is more to life than what is currently on the table. Those better days are still ahead. In all these, it is crucial to keep moving by incorporating the 'how to' formula to the dreams and fantasies. Fantasies and dreams should be guarded and nurtured, for without them the future is gloom which is a perfect breeding ground for procrastination.

Chapter 12

Use the 2-minute rule to stop procrastinating

Some time back, I was battling with procrastination, and I learned that following this simple rule can help even a chronic procrastinator to overcome this weird behavior of putting off tasks over and over again. I call this approach 2-minute rule, and it's geared towards helping you to get started on the tasks you need to do.

Here is the deal...

The majority of the projects you keep on postponing are not difficult to do because you have the abilities to complete those tasks. However, you avoid these tasks due to other reasons, and this implies that you can complete these tasks effectively. The 2-minute rule will help to rule to overcome procrastination and laziness by making it easy for you to begin working.

The 2-minute rule has two parts.

Part one: if the task takes requires less than two minutes, do it now

Are you surprised? How many tasks you have been putting off yet you can get the task done in two minutes or less? Closing a window will take you less than a minute, but you can keep postponing it until you go to bed. Also, taking the garbage out of your house requires less than two minutes but you wait until your house starts stinking, that's when you take it out.

If you follow this rule, you will be able to complete your tasks in time.

Part two: when you begin a new habit, it should not take more than two minutes

"This is weird!" you say. Well, we all know that we can accomplish each goal in two minutes. However, each goal can be started within two minutes – the primary purpose of this rule.

It might sound like this approach is too basic for one's grand life objective but I beg to differ with such perception. The 2-minute rule can work for any goal because of one reason –the physics of real life.

The physics of real life

Sir Isaac Newton, a great physicist, taught that objects at rest tend to remain at rest unless a force is applied to it and objects in motion tend to remain in motion unless an opposing force is applied. This concept is true for humans just like it is for falling objects.

The two-minute rule works for both small and big goals because of the inertia of life – once you start a task, it is easier for you to continue doing it.

Always remember if a task can be done in two minutes or less, do it now, and whenever you begin a new habit, it should not take more than two minutes.

Chapter 13

Keep it going

One of my close friends once told me that the hardest thing about jogging every morning was putting is shoes on. As soon as his shoes were on, he didn't have to worry about the rest of the jogging and didn't feel like stopping. Once you start a project, it is easy to keep going than to give up.

We have discussed so many tips to get you started on your tasks and to ensure that procrastination is gone, keep the work going. Don't dump that book you have been writing just because you are falling short of ideas. Instead of giving up, do all you can too complete each the project successfully. Here are a few tips to help you.

• Track time while working to know how much time it takes you to complete the small tasks in your project. Also, get to know your concentration span (how long it takes your brain to concentrate until it needs a break). With that, you will be able to set an appropriate work schedule with breaks.

• Analyze your motivations in what you are doing and just focus on the benefits of completing the tasks. This will rejuvenate you, and it will be easier for you to work until you complete the project.

• Break down your big projects into small milestones and conquer each at a time.

Apart from keeping your work going, note that your fight against procrastination should not stop. Recall what we learned about how our brains make us procrastinate. Therefore, you should strive to keep everything going for you to succeed in becoming productive.

Conclusion

This appears to be the end of this book, but the start of something more important – 21-day practice plan to end procrastination. You have been reading this book, and now it's time to practice what you have learned.

Keep in mind that you are fighting a beast, and you can't just sit down and expect procrastination to disappear just because you have the 12secrets in your mind. It is not going to work.

Therefore, for the next 21 days, combine various approaches discussed in this book to ensure that you no longer postpone your tasks. Of course, the fight against procrastination will start by understanding yourself, the main roots of procrastination in you, why you procrastinate, and then, utilize the 12 secrets to overcoming this weird behavior.

Remember, ONCE YOU START, NEVER GIVE UP UNTIL THE END.

Thanks for reading this book.

www.ingramcontent.com/pod-product-compliance
Lightning Source LLC
Chambersburg PA
CBHW061236180526
45170CB00003B/1321